DISCARDED

GAYLORD F

Fractions

50133
Jr Non Fic
510

Property Of
Cardington-Lincoln Public Library

Look out for these sections to help you learn more about each topic:

Remember…
This provides a summary of the key concept(s) on each two-page entry. Use it to revise what you have learned.

Word check
These are new and important words that help you understand the ideas presented on each two-page entry.

All of the word check entries in this book are shown in the glossary on page 45. The versions in the glossary are sometimes more extensive explanations.

Book link…
Although this book can be used on its own, other titles in the *Math Matters!* set may provide more information on certain topics. This section tells you which other titles to refer to.

Place value

To make it easy for you to see exactly what we are doing, you will find colored columns behind the numbers in all the examples on this and the following pages. This is what the colors mean:

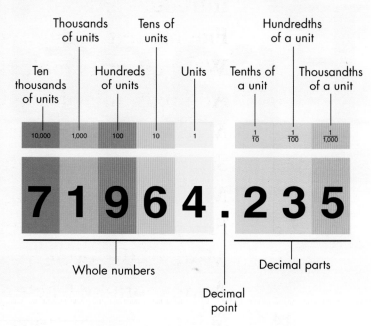

Ten thousands of units · Thousands of units · Hundreds of units · Tens of units · Units · Tenths of a unit · Hundredths of a unit · Thousandths of a unit

10,000   1,000   100   10   1 $\frac{1}{10}$ $\frac{1}{100}$ $\frac{1}{1,000}$

7 1 9 6 4 . 2 3 5

Whole numbers

Decimal point

Decimal parts

Series concept by *Brian Knapp and Duncan McCrae*
Text contributed by *Brian Knapp and Colin Bass*
Design and production by *Duncan McCrae*
Illustrations of characters by *Nicolas Debon*
Digital illustrations by *David Woodroffe*
Other illustrations by *Peter Bull Art Studio*
Editing by *Lorna Gilbert and Barbara Carragher*
Layout by *Duncan McCrae and Mark Palmer*
Reprographics by *Global Colour*
Printed and bound by *LEGO SpA*

First Published in the United States in 1999 by Grolier Educational, Sherman Turnpike, Danbury, CT 06816

Copyright © 1999
Atlantic Europe Publishing Company Limited

All rights reserved. No part of this publication may be reproduced, stored in a retrieval system, or transmitted in any form or by any means – electronic, mechanical, photocopying, recording, or otherwise – without prior permission of the Publisher.

Library of Congress Cataloging-in-Publication Data
Math Matters!
    p. cm.
    Includes indexes.
    Contents: v.1.Numbers — v.2.Adding — v.3.Subtracting — v.4.Multiplying — v.5.Dividing — v.6.Decimals — v.7.Fractions – v.8.Shape — v.9.Size — v.10.Tables and Charts — v.11.Grids and Graphs — v.12.Chance and Average — v.13.Mental Arithmetic
    ISBN 0–7172–9294–0 (set: alk. paper). — ISBN 0–7172–9295–9 (v.1: alk. paper). — ISBN 0–7172–9296–7 (v.2: alk. paper). — ISBN 0–7172–9297–5 (v.3: alk. paper). — ISBN 0–7172–9298–3 (v.4: alk. paper). — ISBN 0–7172–9299–1 (v.5: alk. paper). — ISBN 0–7172–9300–9 (v.6: alk. paper). — ISBN 0–7172–9301–7 (v.7: alk. paper). — ISBN 0–7172–9302–5 (v.8: alk. paper). — ISBN 0–7172–9303–3 (v.9: alk. paper). — ISBN 0–7172–9304–1 (v.10: alk. paper). — ISBN 0–7172–9305–X (v.11: alk. paper). — ISBN 0–7172–9306–8 (v.12: alk. paper). — ISBN 0–7172–9307–6 (v.13: alk. paper).

    1. Mathematics — Juvenile literature. [1. Mathematics.]
I. Grolier Educational Corporation.
QA40.5.M38   1998
510 — dc21   98–7404
                                                          CIP
                                                          AC

This book is manufactured from sustainable managed forests. For every tree cut down at least one more is planted.

Contents

Introduction

$$\frac{3}{4}$$

$$\frac{3}{4}$$

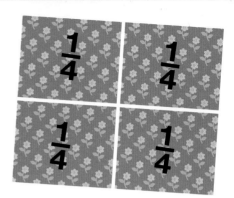

Fractions. This common word comes from the Latin word for "breaking." Fractions are about breaking or splitting things up equally.

We use fractions all the time. We might say, "I'll do half of that job," or "Cut me a quarter of that cake." In fact, as you will see, splitting things into equal parts is so important and useful that a whole system of measurement is based on the idea.

The use of fractions started from the idea that it is very natural to take a length and halve it, then halve each part, then halve each smaller part, and so on. From this we shall see, for example, that a quarter is half of a half.

$$3:5 = \frac{3}{5}$$

$$\frac{3}{4} = 75\%$$

$$\frac{3}{8} = 1\frac{1}{24}$$

$$3 \times \frac{1}{4} = \frac{3}{4}$$

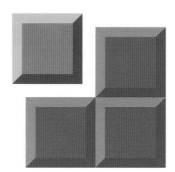

$$\frac{2}{4} - \frac{1}{4} = \frac{1}{4}$$

Fractions are a very practical kind of measure. Fractions also provide a fast way of working with numbers.

To work with fractions, you only need a few simple rules. There are also some smart tricks that save time and allow you to check your answers.

You will find that by following the simple stages in this book, it will be easy to learn all about fractions. Each idea is set out on a separate page, so you can always refer back quickly to an idea if you have forgotten it.

Like all of the books in the *Math Matters!* set, there are many examples. They have been designed to be quite varied because you can use mathematics at any time, any place, anywhere.

$$\frac{18}{54} \text{ or } \frac{2}{6} \text{ or } \frac{1}{3}$$

$$\frac{3}{6} + \frac{2}{6} = \frac{5}{6}$$

Finding out about fractions

A fraction is a part of something. The most common parts are halves – when we split (divide) something into two equal parts – and quarters – when we split something into four equal parts.

One unit

1 or

Halves

$\frac{1}{2}$	$\frac{1}{2}$

Quarters

$\frac{1}{4}$	$\frac{1}{4}$	$\frac{1}{4}$	$\frac{1}{4}$

$\frac{1}{4}$	$\frac{3}{4}$

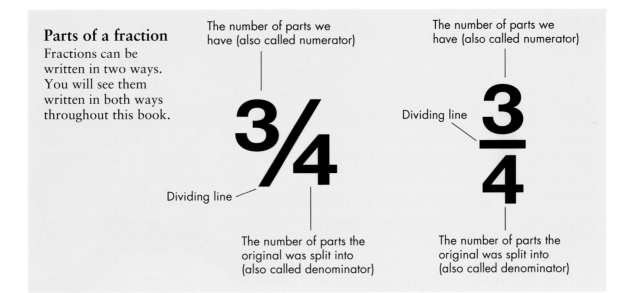

Parts of a fraction

Fractions can be written in two ways. You will see them written in both ways throughout this book.

The number of parts we have (also called numerator)

Dividing line

3/4

The number of parts the original was split into (also called denominator)

The number of parts we have (also called numerator)

Dividing line

$\frac{3}{4}$

The number of parts the original was split into (also called denominator)

Sharing the chocolate bar

Jilly had a chocolate bar. Like most chocolate bars, it was made into a number of blocks joined together.

She broke off (divided up) one of the four sections (fractions). This gave her a piece with three sections, and the fourth piece she was about to eat.

Because Jilly was eating a fourth of the bar, she was eating a quarter. A quarter, one-fourth, is written ¼.

What remained behind was three-fourths (three-quarters), which is written as ¾.

Together the quarter section and the three-quarters section could be fitted together again to make a complete bar.

Remember… Fractions are parts of a whole. The total number of parts is at the bottom of the fraction; the number of equal parts is on the top.

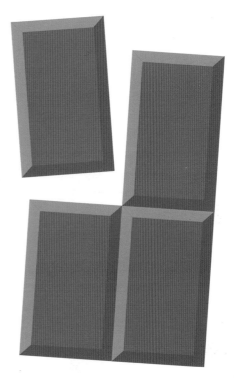

Word check

Denominator: The number written on the bottom of a fraction.

Dividing Line: The line that separates the two number parts of a fraction.

Fraction: A special form of division using a numerator and denominator. The line between the two is called a dividing line.

Numerator: The number written on the top of a fraction.

What quarters look like

You make fractions by dividing something into equal parts. Notice that shape does not affect the fraction because a fraction is simply a *part* of the whole; it tells us nothing about the real size or shape.

You can make fractions by breaking something like a bar of chocolate into equal pieces by size as we saw on page 7.

There are many other ways to make quarters. For example, you could split up a bag of candy by weight using scales. You could also make fractions by volume, splitting a box of orange drink into equal amounts in several glasses. Here are some objects split up to show you the principle.

These two pieces of material have been cut into four equal pieces. Each is a quarter (¼) of the original.

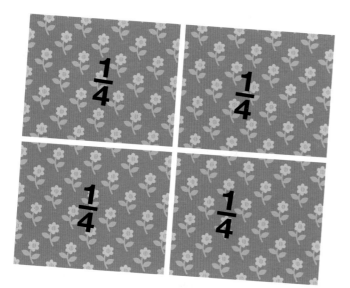

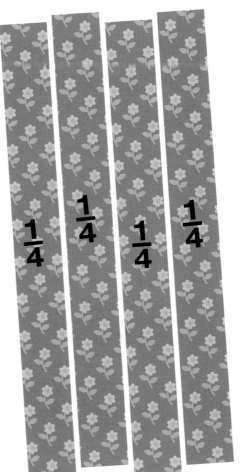

This cake is divided into four equal-sized fractions. To do this, the cut lines make a cross.

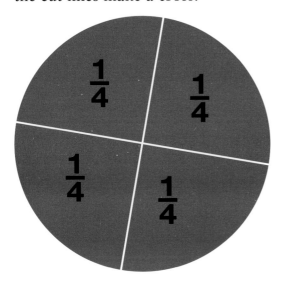

This triangle can be cut into four equal parts, each of which is also a triangle whose sides are all equal. Notice how they fit together.

Book link... For more interesting facts on angles and how shapes fit together, see the book *Shape*, in the *Math Matters!* set.

$\frac{1}{4}$

$\frac{1}{4}$

$\frac{1}{4}$ $\frac{1}{4}$

This is an equilateral triangle.

Here you see four equal portions of orange drink. The words "equal portion" are used to mean fraction in this case because the whole box was poured evenly into each glass so that all glasses contain the same amount.

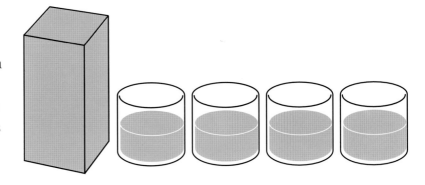

Remember... Each of four equal parts is called one-quarter, or one-fourth. Each of two equal parts is called one-half, but not one-second. All the other fractions are named using ordinal numbers, one-third, one-fifth, and so on.

Word check

Equilateral triangle: A triangle with sides of equal length and angles of equal size. It is the regular triangle.

Ordered numbers: Numbers used for putting things in order, such as first, second, third, fourth, fifth, and so on.

Adding similar fractions

When we create fractions, we create parts of something. Just as we can split something up to make the parts, we can also add the parts together either to make the original again or to make bigger parts.

However, <u>fractions can only be added if they share the same number at the bottom</u>. These kinds of fractions are called similar fractions.

It is easy to see the way adding fractions works using quarters and halves. Just as you can split a half in two to make two quarters, you can fit two quarters together to make a half.

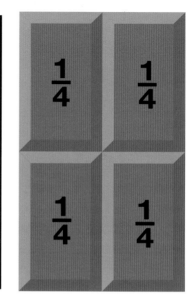

Tempting chocolate

Jilly was feeling particularly greedy because she liked chocolate a lot. So she broke off two quarters to eat.

She was going to eat two quarters or ²⁄₄.

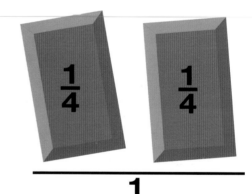

As you can see, this was also one half or ½ (we shall see how to change ²⁄₄ into ½ on page 18):

And of course, this was also exactly what was left: two quarters or one half.

In fact you can see that Jilly had taken two quarters to make a half.

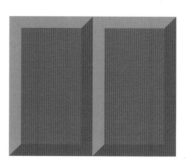

As Jilly thought about whether to eat three quarters, it suddenly occurred to her that she knew how adding fractions worked:

$$\frac{1}{4} + \frac{1}{4} = \frac{1}{2}$$

You start with a unit (1) and then write under it the number of pieces you are splitting (dividing) it into. Since she was dividing it into 4, each piece was the unit (1) divided by 4, hence ¼.

Since she had three of them, she had:

$$\frac{1}{4} + \frac{1}{4} + \frac{1}{4} = \frac{3}{4}$$

Which she worked out simply by adding the top numbers of the fractions together.

And if she had four pieces, she had:

$$\frac{1}{4} + \frac{1}{4} + \frac{1}{4} + \frac{1}{4} = \frac{4}{4}$$

which was the whole bar. So…

$$\frac{4}{4} = 1$$

In fact, she was so impressed with how much she had worked out for herself that she decided to award herself a present and eat the last quarter as well.

So now we can see that

$$\frac{1}{2} + \frac{1}{2} = \frac{2}{2} = 1$$

and

$$\frac{1}{4} + \frac{1}{4} + \frac{1}{4} + \frac{1}{4} = \frac{4}{4} = 1$$

and

$$\frac{1}{4} + \frac{3}{4} = 1$$

Remember… You add similar fractions simply by adding the top numbers this way: ⅕ + ⅖ = ⅗, and ²⁄₇ + ³⁄₇ = ⁵⁄₇.

Word check
Similar fractions: Fractions with the same denominator.

Multiplying fractions

You multiply whole numbers together as a quick way of adding.

Just as **2 + 2 + 2 = 6**, so **3 × 2 = 6**. The same idea also works with fractions. Provided you have similar fractions, you can simply multiply the top of one of the fractions, as this example shows.

Here is one square block of chocolate (1 unit) broken into four.

1 unit

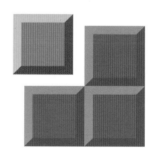

This means that one portion is

$$\frac{1}{4}$$

Three portions are therefore

$$\frac{1}{4} + \frac{1}{4} + \frac{1}{4} = \frac{3}{4}$$

but we can also see that if we took any one of the three fractions (¼) and multiplied it by the number of fractions (3), we would get the same result, like this:

$$3 \times \frac{1}{4} = \frac{3}{4}$$

Here is a further example

Here we are finding four lots of two ninths (this is a quick way of finding ⅔ + ⅔ + ⅔ + ⅔).

$$4 \times \frac{2}{9} = ?$$

Multiply the whole number (4) by the top of the fraction (2). This gives the fraction ⅔.

Multiply the whole number 4 by the top of the fraction

$$\frac{4 \times 2}{9} = \frac{8}{9}$$

Check your answer by adding the tops of the fractions: 2 + 2 + 2 + 2 = 8

Here is another example

Here we are finding three lots of seven twenty-fifths (this is a quick way of finding ⁷⁄₂₅ + ⁷⁄₂₅ + ⁷⁄₂₅).

$$3 \times \frac{7}{25} = ?$$

Multiply the whole number 3 by the top of the fraction

$$\frac{3 \times 7}{25} = \frac{21}{25}$$

Multiply the whole number (3) by the top of the fraction (7). This gives the fraction ²¹⁄₂₅.

Check your answer by adding the tops of the fractions: 7 + 7 + 7 = 21.

Remember... When we multiply fractions by whole numbers, we multiply the top of the fraction by the whole number.

Word check
Unit: 1 of something. A small square shape representing 1.

Smaller and smaller fractions

An easy way to divide something is to halve it and then halve it again and again. This gives you portions that have numbers like **2, 4, 8, 16, 32,** and so on. You simply cut in half again and again until you have the number of fractions you want.

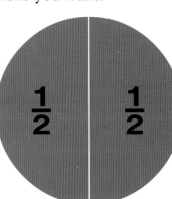

$$\frac{1}{2} + \frac{1}{2} = 1$$

$$\frac{1}{4} + \frac{1}{4} + \frac{1}{4} + \frac{1}{4} = 1$$

$$\frac{1}{8} + \frac{1}{8} + \frac{1}{8} + \frac{1}{8} + \frac{1}{8} + \frac{1}{8} + \frac{1}{8} + \frac{1}{8} = 1$$

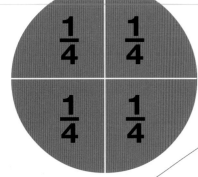

The birthday cake

Salim was having a birthday party, and so a huge cake was baked for the occasion. There were to be **15** guests, and each of them needed to have an equal share of the cake. Nobody could think how to cut the cake into **15** equal portions, but then Salim had a bright idea – cut the cake into **16** and then keep one piece back so that he could have it tomorrow.

So at the party they cut the cake across (making two portions), then across again (making four). Then they cut each quarter to make eight (see page 17) and then cut each eighth to make **16** portions.

But just as Salim was about to put the spare piece away, another friend turned up by surprise. So the extra piece came in handy after all!

$$\frac{1}{16} + \frac{1}{16} + \frac{1}{16} + \frac{1}{16} + \frac{1}{16} + \frac{1}{16} + \frac{1}{16} + \frac{1}{16} + \frac{1}{16} + \frac{1}{16} + \frac{1}{16} + \frac{1}{16} + \frac{1}{16} + \frac{1}{16} + \frac{1}{16} + \frac{1}{16} = 1$$

Remember... Every time we share a piece by cutting it in two, each piece gets smaller, so we <u>multiply the bottom of each fraction by two</u>.

Mixing and matching fractions

You can easily add fractions so long as the number on the bottom of each fraction is the same.

In this example we are combining fractions of two pizzas to give people larger portions and more variety. These are similar things. But you could not add fractions of bricks and apples (unlike things) in this way.

A not-so-quiet meal

Gill was going to give her two children a snack. So she got a pizza out of the freezer and reheated it in her microwave. Then, since there were just two of them, Gill divided the hot pizza neatly into two equal portions, so that each child had a half each. So, $1 = \frac{2}{2}$.

$$1 = \frac{1}{2} + \frac{1}{2}$$

Just as she was about to put the pizza on the plates, the doorbell rang, and two of the children's friends were standing there. Not wishing to be rude, Gill asked them if they would like a pizza snack. So, $1 = \frac{4}{4}$.

Now each of the four children had a smaller snack, so she added a bit of salad to each plate.

$$1 = \frac{1}{4} + \frac{1}{4} + \frac{1}{4} + \frac{1}{4}$$

Then the doorbell rang again. It was four more children. Now Gill had to decide what to do. There were eight people to feed. So she microwaved another pizza.

$2 = \frac{4}{4} + \frac{4}{4}$

$$2 = \frac{1}{4} + \frac{1}{4} + \frac{1}{4} + \frac{1}{4} + \frac{1}{4} + \frac{1}{4} + \frac{1}{4} + \frac{1}{4}$$

However, although the first pizza had pepperoni topping, the second one had cheese topping.

So this is what Gill did: she divided each pizza into 8 and gave a piece of each topping to everyone.

Pepperoni topping

Cheese topping

Each plate then had ⅛ cheese + ⅛ pepperoni. Since there were two pizzas, each person got ¼ of a pizza, so

$$\frac{1}{8} + \frac{1}{8} = \frac{2}{8} = \frac{1}{4}$$

Remember… One eighth of two is the same as one quarter of one. ⅖ and ¼ have the same value. The diagrams show this clearly. They are called equivalent fractions.

Word check
Equivalent fractions: Fractions that have the same value.

Fractions with the same value

Fractions often look different from one another, but they can easily be made to look the same. Here's how.

Halves, quarters, and thirds are all different kinds of fraction because the bottom number, or denominator, is different.

    When you have different fractions, it isn't always easy to know when one fraction is bigger than another. For example, which is the bigger of ⅔ and ¾?

    It is even harder to know which is the bigger of ⅞ and ⅘, for example.

    To get around this problem, we need to make the fractions the same kind. We do this by making the bottom numbers all the same. Then they become similar fractions.

$$\frac{1}{2}$$

This kind of fraction is based on 2. Other fractions of a similar kind are ²⁄₂ and ³⁄₂.

$$\frac{1}{3}$$

This kind of fraction is based on 3. Other fractions of a similar kind are ⅔ and ³⁄₃.

$$\frac{1}{4}$$

This kind of fraction is based on 4. Other fractions of a similar kind are ²⁄₄ and ¾.

Making fractions with the same value

Here are some examples of how we get some different-looking fractions with the same value as ¼:

Multiply the top and bottom by 2 to get ²⁄₈

Multiply the top and bottom by 6 to get ⁶⁄₂₄

$$\frac{1}{4} = \frac{2}{8} = \frac{6}{24}$$

Now look at the fractions that have the same value as ¹²⁄₃₆:

Divide the top and bottom by 2 to get ⁶⁄₁₈

Divide the top and bottom by 4 to get ³⁄₉

Divide the top and bottom by 12 to get ⅓

$$\frac{12}{36} = \frac{6}{18} = \frac{3}{9} = \frac{1}{3}$$

As you can see, many different-looking fractions are really fractions with the same value in disguise.

Making similar fractions

This is done by changing the way we write one or both fractions until they are the same kind of fraction. To do this, <u>we have to make the bottom numbers the same</u>.

Of course, we must not change the <u>value</u> of the fraction. We keep it the same by multiplying the number on top of the fraction, the numerator, by the same number that we multiply the bottom.

For example, if we want to find out which is the bigger number, $\frac{7}{9}$ or $\frac{3}{8}$, we need to make them the same kind of fraction.

$$\text{Is } \frac{7}{9} \text{ bigger than } \frac{3}{8} \text{ ?}$$

Step 1: Multiply the top and bottom of $\frac{7}{9}$ by 8:

$$\frac{7}{9} = \frac{7 \times 8}{9 \times 8} = \frac{56}{72}$$

Step 2: Multiply top and bottom of $\frac{3}{8}$ by 9:

$$\frac{3}{8} = \frac{3 \times 9}{8 \times 9} = \frac{27}{72}$$

Now the fractions are the same kind because the bottom numbers are the same. But because we multiplied each fraction by the same number top and bottom, their values remained the same.

Now it is easy to see that $\frac{56}{72}$ is bigger than $\frac{27}{72}$, so $\frac{7}{9}$ is bigger than $\frac{3}{8}$.

$$\frac{56}{72} \text{ is bigger than } \frac{27}{72} \text{ , so therefore } \frac{7}{9} \text{ is bigger than } \frac{3}{8}$$

Remember... Did you spot how we knew which numbers to multiply by? We used the bottom number of the other fraction. Just check back above to see how it was done.

Word check
Denominator: The number written on the bottom of a fraction.

Numerator: The number written on the top of a fraction.

More of the same, but different

Here are some more examples of fractions that have the same value, although at first they look different. They are also known as <u>equivalent fractions</u>.

Plum picking

Ian had been picking plums. He arranged the plums in rows so they were easier to count. This was his contribution to the picnic the family was going to make.

Each row had **9** plums, and he had **6** rows. So the total was **9 × 6 = 54**.

But in fact he wanted to give some away, so he pushed **2** rows a little apart from the others.

Ian had separated out **2** of the **6** rows, so the top two rows made a collection that was ²/₆ of the total.

Then he separated out another two rows. Now he had another collection that was ²/₆ of the total.

Ian stood back from the plums and saw quite clearly that there were three equal groups. So each group must be one-third of the whole collection, or ⅓.

$$9 \times 6 = 54$$

$$\overset{18 \div 9}{\overbrace{}} \quad \overset{2 \div 2}{\overbrace{}}$$

$\dfrac{18}{54}$ **or** $\dfrac{2}{6}$ **or** $\dfrac{1}{3}$

$$\underset{54 \div 9}{\underbrace{}} \quad \underset{6 \div 2}{\underbrace{}}$$

$\dfrac{18}{54}$ **or** $\dfrac{2}{6}$ **or** $\dfrac{1}{3}$

$\dfrac{18}{54}$ **or** $\dfrac{2}{6}$ **or** $\dfrac{1}{3}$

Ian counted the plums in each group and found there were **18** plums. So each group contained ¹⁸/₅₄ of the total – the equivalent of ⅓.

These fractions all have the same value, just as we saw on the previous page.

More practice

Here are some more equivalent fractions that have the same value. Check that you agree:

$$\frac{7}{21} \quad \text{has the same value as} \quad \overset{7 \times 2}{\frac{14}{42}} \underset{21 \times 2}{} \quad \text{or} \quad \overset{14 \times 2}{\frac{28}{84}} \underset{42 \times 2}{}$$

$$\frac{3}{4} \quad \text{has the same value as} \quad \overset{3 \times 12}{\frac{36}{48}} \underset{4 \times 12}{} \quad \text{or} \quad \overset{3 \times 7}{\frac{21}{28}} \underset{4 \times 7}{}$$

$$\frac{5}{9} \quad \text{has the same value as} \quad \overset{5 \times 9}{\frac{45}{81}} \underset{9 \times 9}{} \quad \text{or} \quad \overset{5 \times 7}{\frac{35}{63}} \underset{9 \times 7}{}$$

Remember... Fractions that look different sometimes have the same value. To find out, try to simplify the fraction by dividing top and bottoms by the same number

Word check
Equivalent fractions: Fractions that have the same value.

Adding unlike fractions

If you have two fractions to add, and their bottom numbers (denominators) are different, you will need to make them of the same kind, or similar fractions.

So, for example, ½ + ⅓ cannot be added until the bottom numbers are the same.

$$\frac{1}{2} + \frac{1}{3} = ?$$

Step 1: Multiply the bottom of the fractions together $2 \times 3 = 6$. This number can be used at the bottom of both fractions and is called the common denominator. In this case **6** is the common denominator.

Step 2: Multiply the top and bottom of each fraction (as we did on page 18) to make the bottom **6**. This will keep the values the same as the original fractions.

Multiplying the top and bottom of ½ by 3 makes:

$$\frac{1 \times 3}{2 \times 3} = \frac{3}{6}$$

Multiplying the top and bottom of ⅓ by 2 makes:

$$\frac{1 \times 2}{3 \times 2} = \frac{2}{6}$$

Now you can add the top numbers, 3 and 2.

$$\frac{3}{6} + \frac{2}{6} = \frac{5}{6}$$

The common denominator

How Bad Boris added unlike fractions to work out his wealth

The old king was fed up. He could not get anyone to marry his four daughters. Finally, he declared that he would divide up his wealth equally among the men who married his daughters.

Baron Boris the Bad married the eldest daughter, Ermintrude, and collected one-quarter (¼) of the king's wealth. But no one would marry any of the other princesses, so ¾ of his wealth remained.

In desperation the king offered to split the ¾ equally among each husband and the person who found his daughters a husband. So, ¾ split **6** ways = ³⁄₂₄ = ⅛.

Quick as a flash, Baron Boris came back with three of his friends to marry the remaining daughters. Now Baron Boris was richer by ¼ + ⅜ of the king's wealth.

How much was that? This is how he figured it out.

He knew they were different kinds of fraction, so his task was to make them the same kind.

He tried multiplying the top and bottom of ¼ by 2:

$$\frac{1}{4} = \frac{1 \times 2}{4 \times 2} = \frac{2}{8}$$

Notice... Because, in this case, one bottom number divides into the other (4 divides into 8), we only have to multiply one fraction.

So $\frac{1}{4} + \frac{3}{8}$ is the same as $\frac{2}{8} + \frac{3}{8}$

Both fractions had an **8** at the bottom, so they were similar fractions.

So the answer was:

$$\frac{2}{8} + \frac{3}{8} = \frac{5}{8}$$

Remember... If you have two different-looking fractions and want to add them, make the bottom the same kind.

Subtracting fractions

Subtracting fractions is simpler once the fractions have been made the same kind, that is, once you have made the bottom numbers the same.

For example, suppose we want to take ¼ from ½. In this case one fraction has the number 2 at the bottom, and the other has 4 at the bottom. We need to change these to be the same.

$$\frac{1}{2} - \frac{1}{4} = \ ?$$

Here we multiply the bottom and also the top of the first fraction (½) by 2 to make it the similar fraction ²⁄₄.

$$\frac{1}{2} = \frac{2 \times 1}{2 \times 2} = \frac{2}{4}$$

Now it is easy; we simply subtract the top numbers, and the answer is ¼.

$$\frac{2}{4} - \frac{1}{4} = \frac{1}{4}$$

Enough flowers?

Here is another example that shows the way fractions are subtracted.

Stephanie was helping her aunt at the flower shop. They had to supply a third (⅓) of their stock to a wedding and half (½) of it to a hotel at the end of the day. But they also had to supply customers waiting in the shop.

They found out how many flowers they could sell in the shop using fractions like this:

The wedding needed ⅓, and the hotel needed ½. Their total stock (1) in fractions was ¹⁄₁.

$$\frac{1}{1} - \frac{1}{3} - \frac{1}{2} = \text{?}$$

So what was left to sell was ¹⁄₁ − ⅓ − ½.

Multiply top and bottom by 6

Multiply top and bottom by 2

Multiply top and bottom by 3

To find what fraction was left to sell, they had to make the fractions of the same kind. <u>They did this by changing them all into sixths</u>, which looks like this:

$$= \frac{6}{6} - \frac{2}{6} - \frac{3}{6}$$

For an explanation of why 6 was used as the bottom number on all the fractions, see page 22.

Now it is easy to subtract:

$$= \frac{6 - 2 - 3}{6}$$

To give the answer:

$$= \frac{1}{6}$$

So they could sell ⅙ of the stock of 900 flowers in the shop.

They worked out ⅙ of 900 by short division and found the answer to be 150.

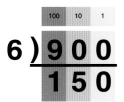

$$6\overline{)900}$$
$$150$$

Provided they did not sell more than 150 before the end of the day, there would be no problem.

Remember... If you want to subtract fractions, then, just like adding, you first have to make the bottoms of each fraction the same number.

Book link... If you are not sure about short division, then look at the book *Dividing*, in the *Math Matters!* set.

Fractions bigger than one

When we add fractions together, we can sometimes end up with more than a whole unit (for example, ⁵⁄₄, when a whole unit is ⁴⁄₄).

If we write these "top-heavy" fractions as whole numbers and fractions, they are called <u>mixed numbers</u>; if we leave them as fractions, then they are called <u>improper fractions</u>.

$$\frac{5}{4} = \frac{1}{4} + \frac{1}{4} + \frac{1}{4} + \frac{1}{4} + \frac{1}{4} = 1\frac{1}{4}$$

Improper fraction   Mixed number

Lots of cake left over

George and Janet prepared lots of food, and the party went really well.

When the party was over, pieces of two cakes and two apple pies remained on the table, as you can see opposite.

Portions had been eaten from both of the cakes and apple pies. You can find out how much was left by adding the fractions that remain like this.

Cherry Cake

To add the two pieces of cherry cake. $\frac{1}{2} + \frac{7}{8}$

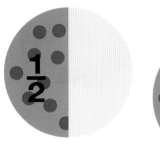

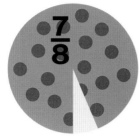

Step 1: Make the bottoms the same. $= \frac{4}{8} + \frac{7}{8}$ $^{1 \times 4}$ $_{2 \times 4}$

Step 2: Add them. $= \frac{11}{8}$

Step 3: Separate any whole numbers. $= \frac{8}{8} + \frac{3}{8}$

Step 4: Write the answer as a whole number and a fraction side by side. $= 1\frac{3}{8}$

Remember... Improper fractions are simply ordinary fractions with a value bigger than **1**.

Apple pies

To add the two pieces of apple pie. $\frac{2}{3} + \frac{3}{8}$

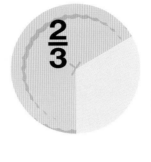

Step 1: Make the bottoms the same. $^{2 \times 8}$ $^{3 \times 3}$ $= \frac{16}{24} + \frac{9}{24}$ $_{3 \times 8}$ $_{8 \times 3}$

Step 2: Add them. $= \frac{25}{24}$

Step 3: Separate any whole numbers. $= \frac{24}{24} + \frac{1}{24}$

Step 4: Write the answer as a whole number and a fraction side by side. $= 1\frac{1}{24}$

Word check
Improper fraction: A fraction whose numerator is bigger than its denominator.
Mixed number: A number made up of an ordinary fraction added to a whole number.

Adding mixed numbers

Very often you find you have improper (top-heavy) fractions or mixed numbers to add.

Adding them is easiest once you have separated out the whole numbers and given all the fractions the same bottom numbers.

Changing improper fractions into mixed numbers

For the calculation using improper (top-heavy) fractions such as:

$$\frac{10}{3} + \frac{27}{6} = ?$$

Step 1: Turn the improper fractions into mixed numbers, and then separate out the whole numbers:

$$\frac{10}{3} = 3\frac{1}{3} = 3 + \frac{1}{3}$$

$$\frac{27}{6} = 4\frac{3}{6} = 4 + \frac{3}{6}$$

So, the calculation for $\frac{10}{3} + \frac{27}{6}$ is now:

$$= 3 + \frac{1}{3} + 4 + \frac{3}{6}$$

Step 2: Add the whole numbers:

$$= 7 + \frac{1}{3} + \frac{3}{6}$$

Step 3: Convert the fractions so they have the same bottoms ($\frac{1}{3} = \frac{2}{6}$):

$$= 7 + \frac{2}{6} + \frac{3}{6}$$

Step 4: Add the whole numbers and the fractions:

$$= 7 + \frac{5}{6} \qquad = 7\frac{5}{6}$$

Adding mixed numbers

Adding mixed numbers is straightforward.
Take the calculation:

$$2\frac{1}{2} + 1\frac{7}{8} = ?$$

Step 1: Separate out the whole numbers and fractions:

$$= 2 + \frac{1}{2} + 1 + \frac{7}{8}$$

Step 2: Add the whole numbers:

$$= 3 + \frac{1}{2} + \frac{7}{8}$$

Step 3: Make the bottoms of the fractions the same ($\frac{1}{2} = \frac{4}{8}$):

$$= 3 + \frac{4}{8} + \frac{7}{8}$$

Step 4: Add the fractions:

$$= 3 + \frac{11}{8}$$

Step 5: Turn the improper fraction into a mixed number ($\frac{11}{8} = 1 + \frac{3}{8}$):

$$= 3 + 1 + \frac{3}{8}$$

Step 5: Add to the whole numbers:

$$= 4\frac{3}{8}$$

Remember... It is easier to add and subtract whole numbers than fractions, so keep to whole numbers as much as you can.

Subtracting mixed numbers

Subtracting mixed numbers is quite easy if you separate the whole numbers from the fractions first. Here's how to do it.

Subtracting the mixed numbers

Graham and Fi wanted to make a drink containing orange juice. They had $3\frac{3}{8}$ bottles of juice. It would need $1\frac{1}{2}$ bottles of juice to make the drink. How much was left at the end?

They needed to work out:

$$3\frac{3}{8} - 1\frac{1}{2} = \ ?$$

Step 1: Make all the bottoms of the fractions the same (change ½ to ⁴⁄₈):

$$= 3 + \frac{3}{8} - 1 - \frac{4}{8}$$

Step 2: Because ⁴⁄₈ is too big to be taken from ³⁄₈, we borrow one of the three whole numbers and write it as ⁸⁄₈:

$$= 2 + \frac{8}{8} + \frac{3}{8} - 1 - \frac{4}{8}$$

Step 3: Subtract the whole numbers (2 − 1 = 1):

$$= \mathbf{1} + \frac{8}{8} + \frac{3}{8} - \frac{4}{8}$$

Step 4: Now work out the fraction:

$$= \mathbf{1} + \frac{8 + 3 - 4}{8}$$

$$= \mathbf{1} + \frac{7}{8}$$

The answer is $= \mathbf{1}\frac{7}{8}$

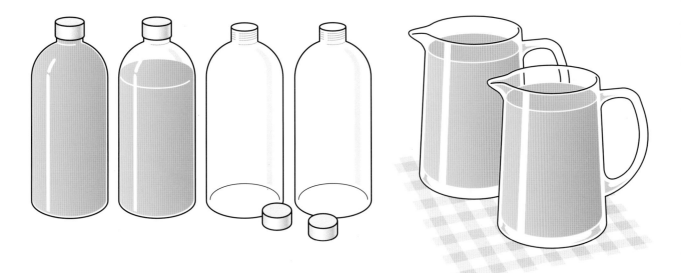

Remember... It is easier to work with mixed numbers than with improper fractions, so convert improper fractions whenever you can.

Book link... To find out more about subtraction, see the book *Subtracting* in the *Math Matters!* set.

Ratios

We use a ratio to compare different numbers of the same thing. For example, we could be thinking about the steepness of a slope. In this case we would be comparing how far you go along to how far you go up. So we are comparing like things (in this case lengths).

In many cases the ratio is disguised by the word "in." So, a slope with a steepness of 1 in 2 is a slope where you go 1 up or down for each 2 you go along.

This can be written down as a ratio 1:2.

1:2

This is the slope

1 unit up or down

2 units along

Geared up

Gears are found in many things, such as bicycles. The gears contain small toothed wheels that mesh with larger toothed wheels. The two wheels are often written as ratios. A gear ratio in the diagram on the right may be written as:

30:50

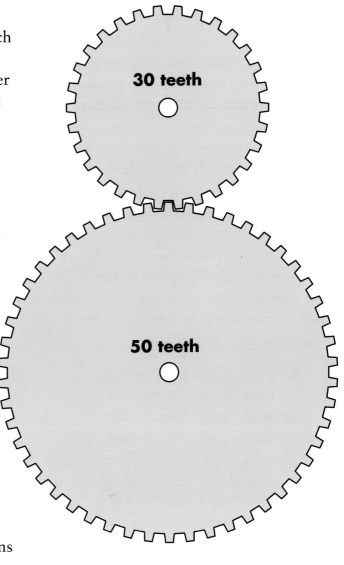

Here's what it means. The first gear wheel on the diagram has 30 teeth, and the second has 50 teeth.

This is actually the same thing as:

3:5

Perhaps this reminds you of fractions that all have the same value even though they look different. In this case the ratio of the gears can also be written as the fraction ⅗.

$$\frac{3}{5}$$

Book link... For more information on slopes and ratios see the book *Dividing* in the *Math Matters!* set.

Remember... Ratios are similar to fractions. They are used to compare similar things, like the number of gear teeth or diameters.

Word check

Ratio: A method of comparing different numbers by placing them on either side of a colon (:); for example, 1:2.

Proportion

We use proportion to compare the numbers in different collections (sets) of things. The numbers in each collection are usually different kinds of things.

Gran's summer drink recipe

Jenny and Pete were confused. They were getting ready for some friends to come that afternoon. They were staying in Canada, where people use metric measures, but their Gran lived in the United States, where they use U.S. measures. She had sent them a recipe for a refreshing cool drink for summer days. It said:

> 1. **Put 1 fl oz of concentrated grapefruit juice in a jug.**
> 2. **Add 1 cup of lemonade.**
> 3. **Add a pint of fresh cold water.**
>
> **Stir it up, add ice cubes, and leave it to stand in a cool shady place until all the ice has melted.**
>
> **Then serve immediately.**

The only jug they had was a 1-liter jug. How could they measure a pint of water in a liter jug? How big a cup should they use? What is a "fl oz"?

They went to the library to look it up. They found these tables in a book.

This seemed a hard problem. But in fact they didn't even need a calculator or a pint jug or even a liter jug. This is because they could use proportion as shown on page 36.

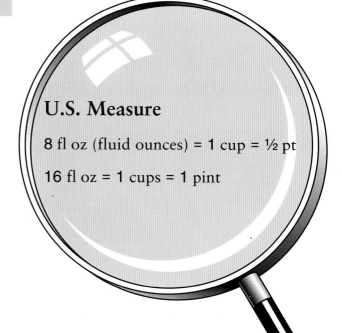

U.S. Measure

8 fl oz (fluid ounces) = 1 cup = ½ pt

16 fl oz = 1 cups = 1 pint

Using proportion

First they needed to change everything into the same kind of measure. They chose to use U.S. fluid ounces.

These are the fluid ounces of the ingredients:

Grapefruit concentrate		=	**1 fl oz**
Lemonade	**1 cup**	=	**8 fl oz**
Water	**1 pint**	=	**16 fl oz**

Now they knew the <u>ratios</u> of the ingredients:

Grapefruit concentrate 1 : Lemonade 8 : Water 16

But they still didn't have anything that measured fluid ounces. So this is where <u>proportion</u>, or ratio, came in.

They used one of their own glasses to measure out the ingredients in the same <u>proportion</u> as Gran's recipe into a big bowl: 1 glass of juice, 8 glasses of lemonade, 16 glasses of water.

So they had **1 + 8 + 16 = 25 glasses** of drink.

Now they could see how to make 50 glasses of drink by increasing everything proportionally by 2.

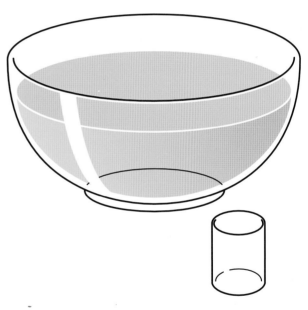

Grapefruit concentrate 2 : Lemonade 16 : Water 32

or whatever <u>proportion</u> they wanted.

Remember… All the ratios had to be in the same units before the drinks could be mixed in proportional amounts.

Word check

Ratio: A method of comparing different numbers by placing them on either side of a colon (:); for example, 1:2.

Proportion: A comparative share in something.

Units: A word used with measurement. For example, metric units.

Percent

Percentage, %, means "for each hundred." Percentages are a quick way of comparing sizes.

Percentages are numbers like the tops of fractions in which the bottom numbers have all already been fixed as 100. This makes them very easy to compare.

Mathematicians use a special symbol, %, to mean percent or "/100."

To make a fraction into a percentage, all we do is multiply the top (numerator) by 100 and then divide by the bottom (denominator) and add a % sign.

$$\text{Percentage} = \frac{\text{Numerator} \times 100}{\text{Denominator}} = \%$$

In this example we convert the fraction ¼ into a percentage.

Step 1: Multiply 1 by 100:

$$\frac{1}{4} \times 100 = \frac{100}{4}$$

Step 2: Divide by 4, then add the % (percent) sign:

$$= 25\%$$

Here are some common fractions written as percentages.

½ as a percentage:

$$\frac{1}{2} \times 100 = \frac{100}{2} = 50\%$$

¾ as a percentage:

$$\frac{3}{4} \times 100 = \frac{300}{4} = 75\%$$

⅝ as a percentage:

$$\frac{5}{8} \times 100 = \frac{500}{8} = 62\tfrac{1}{2}\%$$

⅓ as a percentage:

$$\frac{1}{3} \times 100 = \frac{100}{3} = 33\tfrac{1}{3}\%$$

⅔ as a percentage:

$$\frac{2}{3} \times 100 = \frac{200}{3} = 66\tfrac{2}{3}\%$$

Remember... Some calculators have a percent key. Press **1**, then ÷, then **3**, then % to check the percentage equal to ⅓ (**33.3%**).

Word check

Per: A Latin word meaning "for each." We see it in words like percent (for each hundred).

Percent: A number followed by the % symbol means the number divided by 100. It is a way of writing a fraction.

Converting percentages to fractions

We need to be able to convert between fractions and percentages easily. Here is how it is done.

To turn a percentage into a fraction

To turn a percentage into a fraction, <u>divide</u> it by **100**, and then reduce it to the simplest possible fraction.

For example,

$$10\% = \frac{10}{100}$$

The top and bottom can be divided by **10**, so $^{10}\!/_{100}$ simplifies to $^{1}\!/_{10}$.

$$\frac{10}{100} = \frac{1}{10}$$

More examples

To turn **20%** into a fraction, divide by **100**, then simplify by division:

$$20\% = \frac{20}{100} = \frac{2}{10} = \frac{1}{5}$$

$$\overset{20 \div 10}{} \qquad \overset{2 \div 2}{}$$

$$\underset{100 \div 10}{} \qquad \underset{10 \div 2}{}$$

To turn **60%** into a fraction, divide by **100**, then simplify by division:

$$60\% = \frac{60}{100} = \frac{6}{10} = \frac{3}{5}$$

$$\overset{60 \div 10}{} \qquad \overset{6 \div 2}{}$$

$$\underset{100 \div 10}{} \qquad \underset{10 \div 2}{}$$

Sometimes you can't reduce it at all, such as in the case of **63%**:

$$63\% = \frac{63}{100}$$

And then you simply have to leave it as it is.

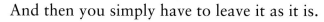

To unmix percentages and fractions

Sometimes fractions and percentages get mixed up. You need to get rid of the fraction first. Then it can be simplified:

$$62\tfrac{1}{2}\% = \frac{62\tfrac{1}{2}}{100} = \frac{125}{200} = \frac{5}{8}$$

$62\tfrac{1}{2} \times 2$ $125 \div 25$

100×2 $200 \div 25$

This is a mixed fraction

Percentages to mixed numbers

Sometimes percentages are greater than **100**. Converting them to fractions then makes a fraction bigger than **1**.

For example, **125%** is equal to ⅝:

$$125\% = \frac{125}{100} = \frac{5}{4}$$

$125 \div 25$

$100 \div 25$

⅝ can either be left like this as an improper fraction or converted further into a mixed number, 1¼:

$$\frac{5}{4} = 1\tfrac{1}{4}$$

Remember... Percentages are often widely used instead of fractions. To convert to a fraction, just divide the percentage by **100**.

Book link... Find out about changing between decimals and fractions in the book *Decimals* in the *Math Matters!* set.

Percent more

Percentage more means the extra percentage added to the original.

You often see signs on the items in stores saying that you are offered so much percent more. Here is an example.

25% extra free on your cornflakes

25% of the original amount added

25% of the original amount

The original amount

The new amount is the original amount of cornflakes + ¼ of the original,

$$100\% = \frac{4}{4}$$

or 25% more.

$$25\% = \frac{1}{4}$$

That is, for every four cornflakes you pay for, you get one more free.

$$= \frac{4}{4} + \frac{1}{4} = \frac{5}{4} = 125\%$$

Lucky Jim

Here is an example of "percent more" with a twist. See how we can use the fraction to find out what discount we have been given.

Jim set off for the supermarket intent on buying 42 burgers for a barbecue. He also expected to buy them in sealed packs of 6. On arrival Jim finds that burgers are on special offer, with 7 burgers to a pack instead of six.

Each pack contains 7 burgers, so he buys 6 of these special packs (6 packs × 7 burgers = 42).

How much has he saved? He expected to pay for seven packs and has paid for only six.

He has saved ⅐ th of the money he expected to pay. His calculator shows 14.3.

$$\frac{1}{7} = 14.3\%$$

Calculator check
1. Enter 1
2. Press division sign (/ or ÷)
3. Enter 7
4. Press % sign (%)
   (Answer reads 14.28571, which on rounding is 14.3%)

So the free burger is worth a discount of a seventh, or 14.3%.

Remember... Percentages are always based on an "original amount," the amount we started with, which is given the value of 100.

Word check
Discount: The amount of money the price is reduced by, often given as a percentage of the original price.
Rounding: Making a number simpler.

Percent less

Percentages are always based on an original amount.
   To find out the answer to a percent less problem, we need to multiply the original amount by the percentage, then take it away from the original amount.

So, for example, to work out 400 less 20%.

Step 1: First write 20% as a fraction:

$$20\% = \frac{20}{100}$$

Step 2: Then multiply the fraction by the original amount:

$$= \frac{20}{100} \times 400 = \frac{8,000}{100}$$

Step 3: Then simplify:

$$= 80$$

So 80 is 20% of 400.

Step 4: Finally, take this from the original:

$$400 - 80 = 320$$

Great Aunt Freda's spending money gets less and less

When Great Aunt Freda went away on her summer holiday, she decided to buy 100 tokens to use in a slot machine. For 3 days she lost 25% of the tokens <u>that remained</u> every day and never won anything. How many tokens did she have left at the end of 3 days?

If Freda lost 25% of her tokens the first day, then she had 75 tokens remaining, or 75% of the original:

$$25\% = \frac{25}{100}$$

$$\frac{100}{100} - \frac{25}{100} = \frac{75}{100} = 75 \text{ tokens}$$

The second day her starting amount was 75 tokens. She lost 25% of 75 tokens,

$$75 \times \frac{25}{100} = \frac{75}{4} = 19 \text{ tokens}$$

which is only 19 tokens. This meant she had

$$75 - 19 = 56$$

56 tokens left, which was her starting amount for the third day.

The same thing happened the third day, so she lost:

$$56 \times \frac{25}{100} = \frac{56}{4} = 14 \text{ tokens}$$

Which meant she had 42 tokens left.

$$56 - 14 = 42$$

Freda, like every other sensible person, knew that you can never win against a slot machine because they are designed to make you lose the same percentage every time on average.

After 3 days, the end of the holiday, Freda still had 42 tokens left.

So, far from spending all the tokens she started with, Freda could expect to have 42 tokens left.

Remember... Great Aunt Freda lost 25% each day. That was 25% of what she started with each day. Her starting amount became less each day. That is why she lost smaller and smaller amounts.

Book link... Find out about averages in the book *Chance and Averages* in the *Math Matters!* set.

What symbols mean

Here is a list of the common math symbols together with an example of how they are used. You will find this list in each of the *Math Matters!* books, so that you can turn to any book if you want to look up the meaning of a symbol.

— Between two numbers this symbol means "subtract" or "minus." In front of one number it means the number is negative. In Latin *minus* means "less."

= The symbol for equals. We say it "equals" or "makes." It comes from a Latin word meaning "level" because weighing scales are level when the amounts on each side are equal.

+ The symbol for adding. We say it "plus." In Latin *plus* means "more."

× The symbol for multiplying. We say it "multiplied by" or "times."

$$(8 + 9 - 3) \times \frac{2}{5} = 5.6$$

( ) Parentheses. You do everything inside the parentheses first. Parentheses always occur in pairs.

—, /, and **÷** Three symbols for dividing. We say it "divided by." A pair of numbers above and below a / or – make a fraction, so ⅖ or $\frac{2}{5}$ is the fraction two-fifths.

■ This is a decimal point. It is a dot written after the units when a number contains parts of a unit as well as whole numbers. This is the decimal number five point six or five and six-tenths.

Glossary

Terms commonly used in this book.

Denominator: The number written on the bottom of a fraction.

Discount: The amount of money the price is reduced by, often given as a percentage of the original price.

Dividing Line: The line that separates the two number parts of a fraction. It is sometimes written horizontally — and sometimes sloping / . It is also called the division line. It is one of the signs mathematicians use for dividing. The other is ÷.

Equilateral triangle: A triangle with sides of equal length and angles of equal size. It is the regular triangle.

Equivalent fractions: Fractions that have the same value.

Fraction: A special form of division using a numerator and denominator. The line between the two is called a dividing line.

Improper fraction: A fraction whose numerator is bigger than its denominator.

Mixed number: A number made up of an ordinary fraction added to a whole number.

Numerator: The number written on the top of a fraction.

Ordered numbers: Numbers used for putting things in order, such as first, second, third, fourth, fifth, and so on. Also called "ordinal numbers." *See* Unordered numbers.

Per: A Latin word meaning "for each." We see it in words like percent (for each hundred).

Percent: A number followed by the % symbol means the number divided by 100. It is a way of writing a fraction.

Place value: The value of a digit due to its position in a number. For example, the value of a number placed to the left of a decimal point has a value in the units; a number placed two digits to the left of a decimal point has a value in the tens, and so on.

Proportion: A comparative share in something.

Ratio: A method of comparing different numbers by placing them on either side of a colon (:); for example, 1:2. The numbers must be measured in the same units. The order of the numbers matters. A ratio is like a fraction.

Rounding: Making a number simpler.

Similar fractions: Fractions with the same denominator.

Unit: 1 of something. A small square shape representing 1.

Units: A word used with measurement. For example, metric units.

Unordered numbers: Numbers used for counting when the order does not matter, such as one, two, three, four, five, and so on. Also called "cardinal numbers" or "counting numbers." *See* Ordered numbers.

Set index

USING THE SET INDEX

The 13 volumes in the *Math Matters!* set are:

Volume number	Title
1:	**Numbers**
2:	**Adding**
3:	**Subtracting**
4:	**Multiplying**
5:	**Dividing**
6:	**Decimals**
7:	**Fractions**
8:	**Shape**
9:	**Size**
10:	**Tables and Charts**
11:	**Grids and Graphs**
12:	**Chance and Average**
13:	**Mental Arithmetic**

An example entry:

Index entries are listed alphabetically.

numerator **6:** 32, 33; **7:** 7, 36

The volume number is shown in bold for each entry. In this case the index entry for "numerator" is found in two titles: **Decimals** and **Fractions**.

The page references in each volume are shown in regular type. In this case pages 32 and 33 of the title **Decimals** and pages 7 and 36 of the title **Fractions**.